IMPACT
GENERATION

YOUTH ACTIVISM FOR
A BETTER TOMORROW

**COMPILED BY ANGELA R. EDWARDS
WITH CONTRIBUTIONS FROM
TODAY'S YOUTH**

IMPACT GENERATION

YOUTH ACTIVISM FOR A BETTER TOMORROW

Compiled By Angela R. Edwards

With Contributions From

(listed by appearance):

Alexis Miller

Ahmir Thompson

Aniyah Williams

Arianna Mickens

Cynsere Williams

McKinzie Baker

Paige Ivory

Righteous Williams

Pearly Gates Publishing LLC
INSPIRING CHRISTIAN AUTHORS TO BE AUTHORS

Pearly Gates Publishing, LLC, Harlem, GA (USA)

Impact Generation:
Youth Activism for a Better Tomorrow

Copyright © 2024
Angela R. Edwards

ISBN 13: 978-1-948853-75-0

Scripture references are used with permission from Zondervan via Biblegateway.com. Public Domain.

For information and bulk ordering, contact:
Pearly Gates Publishing, LLC
Angela Edwards, CEO
P.O. Box 639
Harlem, GA 30814
PearlyGatesPublishing@gmail.com

[v]

DEDICATION

To the resilient youth of today, may you always know that the adults in your lives stand beside you with unwavering support and understanding. We see your struggles, we empathize with your challenges, and we believe in your strength. Our hearts are filled with nothing but prayers for the brightest and most fulfilling outcomes in your lives. You are not alone, and we are here to uplift, encourage, and stand by you through it all.

With love and unwavering faith in your potential,
this book is dedicated to you.

ACKNOWLEDGMENTS

First, I give all honor and glory to **GOD**, who is the Head of my life. I am grateful for His gifts and His inspiration to bring youths together to sow seeds of hope, encouragement, and love into others—young and old alike.

I want to thank the Foreword Writer, **Alexis Miller**, for sharing her gift and testimony with us. When I reached out to the Founder of Positive Express, Ms. Tosha Dearbone, and asked if she had anyone in mind who would pick up the mantle to write the Foreword and run with it, she said, "I know JUST the young lady," without hesitation. I am pleased to say that Alexis did not disappoint. What a powerful young woman of God she is!

To the seven youth authors who remained involved in this project from start to finish—**Ahmir Thompson, Aniyah Williams, Arianna Mickens, Cynsere Williams, McKinzie Baker, Paige Ivory, and Righteous Williams**—*THANK YOU* for your fantastic and relatable stories! I applaud your work ethic and willingness to be transparent with the world. Your stories are sure to help others see that they are not alone in their struggles. May you **ALL** be blessed today and always.

To the **Parents and Guardians**: Thank you for guiding your youths through each piece of this anthology. Your sticktoitiveness reflects your heart's desire to see things through to the end, and I pray your youths appreciate your gentle nudging to adhere to their commitments in the days and years to come.

I'm giving a special shout-out to **Marlowe Scott**, Owner of M.R.S. Inspirations. Early in the process of compiling this book, she had the idea to purchase a special gift for each of the youth authors. One thing I know for certain is that Marlowe, lovingly known as "Mom Marlowe" to *MANY*, encourages and supports our youths at every turn. As her daughter, I can attest to how she has encouraged and supported me throughout the years, so it was no surprise that she stepped up with an amazing offer to further empower the youth authors. **THANK YOU, MOM!** I love and appreciate you!

Last but not least, I want to thank each and every single person who will read this book and take from it what is for **YOU**. May the stories contained herein help you, your family, and your peers through the unknown days ahead. Be strong. Be courageous. Help others by sharing this book with them.

God Bless, one and all!

INTRODUCTION

t's the 21st century. The voices of today's youths have become increasingly profound, resonating with wisdom, compassion, and a desire for positive change. This anthology—*Impact Generation: Youth Activism for a Better Tomorrow*—presents a collection of short stories penned by youths who have embarked on remarkable journeys to instigate a transformative impact among their peers, within their homes, and throughout their communities. Their narratives symbolize adolescents' pioneering spirits and exceptional endeavors in the modern era, encapsulating the essence of their impactful experiences and the ripple effect of their actions.

The stories within the pages of this book serve as testaments to the pioneering narratives woven by young people who refuse to be confined by the stereotypes of adolescence. Each story is evidence of the resilience, empathy, and innovation that defines the young authors as they navigate the complexities of life in the 21st century. Through the transparency of their truths, they challenge the status quo and redefine the traditional notions of youth empowerment and advocacy.

The exceptional endeavors of the youths unfold within the pages of this book, showcasing their unwavering commitment to catalyzing change. Each of the stories herein demonstrates an extraordinary capacity to effect positive differences. Their endeavors exemplify the innate potential embedded within them to lead by example and inspire meaningful transformation.

The significance of the stories in *Impact Generation: Youth Activism for a Better Tomorrow* extends beyond the individual narratives, resonating with a collective call to act. Their stories illuminate the potential of today's youth to be catalysts for positive change, all while dispelling misconceptions and showcasing the power of youthful determination. In an era marked by complex global challenges, their efforts stand as beacons of hope, illustrating the impact that can only be achieved through empathy, innovation, and a steadfast belief in the possibility of a better world today. . . and tomorrow. Their experiences serve as a reminder that every individual, regardless of age, possesses the ability to initiate those difficult conversations and that the collective force of youthful determination can ignite profound and lasting change.

As you immerse yourself in the true stories presented in *Impact Generation: Youth Activism for a Better Tomorrow*, you are granted a glimpse into the future shaped by the unwavering commitment of today's youth to create a more inclusive, compassionate, and sustainable society. Their stories not only inspire but also demonstrate the potential within each of them to offer a compelling narrative of hope and possibility and shape a brighter future for generations to come.

Angela R. Edwards, Compiler

FOREWORD

BY ALEXIS MILLER

Alexis
Miller

L ife hasn't been a dream for me. I've been hurt so many times, I thought nothing would ever hurt me again. It seems as though I was wrong. At times, I suffer from depression. I know how it is to be picked on and want to give up on life.

As a young writer, I feel I can connect with many other teens my age. As a teenager, I've witnessed other teens being picked on because of their living situation (I am one of those teens). For a while, I had no place to sleep and lived in some very cruel environments. Another thing I have seen is teens with a lot of built-up emotional hurt and trauma. Some are good at hiding it, but there are those who cannot hold it in because of how fragile they are.

My point is this: You can't pick on someone and expect them just to let you continue to hurt them. One day, you're going to come up against someone who is so hurt and so broken that they will release all that built-up anger on you.

Think about it. . . How would you feel if your life was already challenging and traumatic, just to have someone decide that you would be the one to get picked on for the clothes you wear, the shoes on your feet, or even the way you smell or talk? I don't believe that you would like it for one millisecond. Stop for just one moment and put yourself in their shoes. After all, you have no idea what is happening to them at home or what might be going through their mind. That person you're picking on could be depressed or, worse yet, suicidal. If they were suicidal and got fed up with your teasing and bullying and then took their own life, how would you be able to look at yourself?

If you are the one being bullied, don't let them bring you down. At the end of the day, you must know your worth. You are strong. You are powerful. Keep your head up, and don't allow yourself to be the subject of someone's ridicule. Show them their words can't hurt you, even when they do. In due time, that bully will see how their words aren't hurting you, and they'll back off. Although it may sound easier said than done, don't let anyone know that they're hurting you because it gives them the power to keep hurting you—and they'll think it's okay to bully others.

I wrote a poem for all of you who may be going through something. It is meant to encourage you and let you know you aren't alone in anything you do. If you think you are alone at any point, you must remember there are people in the world who are likely going through the same thing. I hope you are encouraged to keep on going and never give up on anything you do. My poem is titled "Never Alone."

Never Alone

You're never alone.

It's okay to be in your zone.

Just know this life is like a stone,

But its words won't break you to the bone.

Just know you matter;

Keep climbing this never-ending ladder.

Don't give up in life,

Even when others' words are cutting you like a knife.

Just know you're loved,

Especially by The One above.

You're perfect the way you are.

I know this walk may seem too far,

But don't take a bully's words to heart,

To the point where they break you apart.

This journey called 'life' may be hard,

And sometimes you may play the wrong card,

But just know it's okay

And put a smile on your day.

Just be yourself

And find the best in your inner self.

Find the one to put your trust in,

And pour out your feelings and let them listen.

Know not to trust everyone so much.

Don't make everyone your crutch,

Because in the process, you may hurt them,

But still remember: You're a gem.

Enjoy your life while you can,

And if you're doing better, just know I'm your number one fan.

Everyone matters in this world.

We're all our own shining pearl.

Keep your head held high,

And show your haters that you still thrive.

Don't let your haters bring your mood down

And turn your smiling day into a frown.

They're just jealous and want to get in your head.

Just remember what this author said:

"You're perfect the way you are.

So, go ahead and bandage up that scar."

I wrote that poem because I was being picked on about my clothes and even how I smelled. It was tough growing up, thinking that I was never good enough. I was always told that I was a "very nasty and disgusting person."

As I was growing up, I was with my father for a couple of years. My father was a very strong man who would physically hit me and emotionally abuse me in many ways. I always tried to convince him that I didn't do anything, but that only made him hurt me more. I was also mentally abused by him. To this day, I don't have a good relationship with him. He always says, "I'm doing better," but then he goes on to do the same thing over and over again. I don't know how he expects to come back into my life after all he has put me through, but I refuse to allow his actions to predict how I will be in the future. Staying with my father caused me to feel as though I was the problem, especially considering my mother also wasn't in the picture.

Growing up without my parents in my life is hard and makes me feel like I've always been "the problem." However, as I've grown up, I've realized that I was never the problem—it was them and their mindset. Now, they're missing out on seeing their baby girl grow and become stronger and wiser. I'm going to show them that hurting me didn't make me give up. Instead, it made me stronger and more aware of how life truly is. So, thank you, Mom and Dad, for making me see that I was never the issue.

I AM THE SOLUTION TO HELPING THOSE WHO ARE GOING THROUGH THE SAME THINGS I DID!

Always remember: You are enough—no matter what you are going through. You are worthy. You are strong. You are never alone. Things will get better, and you will become stronger as life continues. As the song says, "What doesn't kill you makes you stronger!" Always hold your head high and know there are people who truly understand your situation and have likely gone through the same things.

Although this world can be complicated and scary, know you will be okay. Don't let anyone get under your skin.

Keep smiling.

Keep a positive mindset.

Keep going.

Keep growing.

And keep showing your haters that you're not as weak as they think you are.

Alexis Miller

TABLE OF CONTENTS

MINDFULNESS EXERCISES, MEDITATION TECHNIQUES, AND RELAXATION ACTIVITIES FOR TEENS

I've Learned to Let "It" Go

BY AHMIR THOMPSON

My life as a youth in today's society is much like that of other youths: It's way too hard! It seems like I am constantly arguing with somebody because I can't express myself any other way to be understood. As if that isn't enough, the added pressures of doing chores at home and everything else on my mind weigh heavily on me.

I had to stop and ask myself, *"What is making me so* **annoyed** *with everything and everyone?"*

The main thing I'm dealing with is issues in school. You see, I'm a big boy who gets bullied by others about my size. *Can I* **please** *catch a break?* Although it's who I am and have always been, it hurts to be bullied about something I can't control. I've lost people I thought were my friends along the way, but I still push through. I find myself stressed out and overthinking everything, too. When I react or act out, it causes problems, and I begin to think bad thoughts. The stress I endure is just too much! The bullying, keeping my grades up in school, and life at home are just **TOO** much sometimes.

I've learned how to escape it all when it becomes overwhelming: I rap freestyle to release the pain—especially when people make racist jokes about me. Although those hurt feelings follow me home, I applaud myself for turning those negatives into positives in a constructive way the moment they occur. I've also gotten rid of my phone and social media, which helped to put a stop to **a lot** of the bullying I dealt with. You know, now that I think about it, I actually like school now more than ever. I've learned to let things go and just relax (I still rap, though)!

Editor's Note on Bullying:

Today's youth encounter a myriad of challenges, from academic pressures and social media scrutiny to mental health struggles and bullying. In the face of those obstacles, it is crucial to cultivate an environment where young people can find support.

Bullying, in particular, is an ever-present issue that affects countless youths, leaving long-lasting impacts on their mental and emotional well-being. However, it's important to acknowledge that the story of bullying is not one-sided. While it undoubtedly brings about negative consequences, there are also instances where individuals have emerged from those challenges with resilience and strength—much like Ahmir.

Ahmir faced severe bullying throughout his school years but found the inner strength to overcome his harrowing experience by focusing on something that he loves: rapping freestyle. Despite enduring relentless taunts, he has emerged with a message of hope for those facing similar challenges. His story stands as a testament to the resilience that can blossom in the face of adversity.

Ahmir's open and honest account about being bullied is a complex tapestry woven with both darkness and light. While there are, indeed, profound negative impacts, his story should remind us all of the human spirit's capacity to rise above adversity. As peers and adults alike, it is imperative that we approach the issue with empathy, understanding, and a commitment to fostering environments where our youth can flourish—free from bullying's shadow.

Parents, we hold the power to shape the environment in which today's youth grow and thrive. Supporting our youth is a collective responsibility that demands tangible action. Let's actively listen to their concerns, offer guidance without judgment, and advocate for mental health resources in educational institutions.

I Almost Died

BY ANIYAH WILLIAMS

Aniyah
Williams

almost died. At the height of the COVID-19 pandemic in late 2021, I wasn't feeling well. My mommy took me to the local children's hospital, where I was diagnosed with MIS-C (Multisystem Inflammatory Syndrome in Children)—a life-threatening illness. My condition quickly worsened, so I was immediately transported by ambulance to Texas Children's Hospital, where my mother was assured that I would receive the best care possible for my at-the-time very rare condition.

Honestly, I don't remember much about the experience because I was intubated—meaning I was placed into a coma-like state—for two days and then intubated for a total of five days. Although I wasn't fully aware of all that was happening around me, I do know that my mom was right by my side, day in and day out. She later explained to me that she was unable to come and go as she pleased because the hospital was under strict COVID-19 protocols, so she couldn't even step foot outside of the hospital without having to leave my side for 24 hours. My mommy never complained, though. She had the support of my stepfather and grandparents to help keep her level-headed and strong for me throughout the entire ordeal.

My dad also came to spend time with me while I was in the hospital. He's a truck driver and was out of the state when I was admitted, but he took the time to fly into Houston to be by my side as well. His visit came at the later part of my hospital stay. By then, I could move around a little and eat on my own. I recall him spending a lot of money ordering food because I refused to eat what the hospital served. Yes, I am spoiled like that. (LOL!)

When I was able to function on my own again, I remember the doctors telling me I would likely never play sports or do any strenuous activities. Apparently, MIS-C was so rare at the time that they weren't sure how many of my bodily functions would return to the before-COVID state.

I refused to accept that as my fate. I was always active before MIS-C, and I believed in my heart it would be the same after MIS-C.

Once I entered middle school, I tried out for my school's cheerleading team. Guess what? I MADE THE TEAM! But, after going to the doctor's office for follow-up testing and a physical, the cardiologist (heart doctor) told me that my heart was still beating irregularly and that she couldn't clear me to participate in cheerleading. I was so upset about that report on my health.

My mom talked to the cheer coaches, asking if there were any other tasks I could do for the team, and they stated I could act as a manager. I declined the offer because I was still upset about being unable to cheer for my school.

For the next year, I went to doctor appointments after doctor appointments. Time and again, I was told my heart was not strong enough to add any strain to it. Can you imagine how I felt when I was FINALLY told I could participate in school activities? I was so excited! Remember I said that I believed in my heart my life would return to normal after MIS-C?

Well. . .

As of the time of this writing, I am now in 7th grade. I was able to try out for the cheerleading team again, and once again, I made the team! Shortly after, I was scheduled for another stress test with my cardiologist, and I passed with flying colors. I was then ready to try out for an even more physical sport, so I set my sights on running track for my school. Guess what? I MADE THAT TEAM, TOO!

I now participate in two extra-curricular activities: cheerleading and track. In cheerleading, I'm a choreographer. After much practice, the first time I ever ran track, I made first place and am heading to district finals. Oh! I can't forget to mention that I am working toward being on my school's volleyball team for the 2024-2025 school year.

I share my comeback story to show other youths that GOD always has the final say. The doctors counted me out. The doctors said it was likely I would never live a normal life again. Those same doctors are amazed by my comeback!

I'm very happy about my recovery from a sickness that could have taken my life. I'm also very grateful for my mom and her entire support system throughout the whole ordeal. My mom was interviewed by our local FOX news station about me and my MIS-C diagnosis. You can view the replay here: https://www.youtube.com/watch?v=NDpdDL9U1yA

I know I was prayed for daily, and God's angels protected me from crossing over into death's door. Today, I am glad I can participate in activities with my friends, and although my younger sisters often drive me crazy, I am blessed to have them in my life. They help to keep my heart healthy! (Smiles)

Awakening Warrior: Overcoming the Battlefield of Life

BY ARIANNA MICKENS

Arianna Mickens

W hen I was a young warrior, I did and experienced a LOT of things that many worldly girls go through without the Lord Jesus. Suicidal thoughts? Yes. Anxiety? Yes. Bullying? Yes. Cursing, disobedience, and seizures? Yes, yes, and yes.

Jesus is the mighty Drill Sergeant of my life. When I lived without Him, I often found myself in situations that I'd try to fix on my own. I knew God but only knew Him in the way I saw Him in my natural eye. I never acted upon the Spirit of the Lord. Before getting to know Him for myself, my days looked like this:

Get up, go to the battlefield, pray, train, and go, go, go.

Although I am still young, I have learned throughout my experiences that without Jesus, there's nothing. Most pointedly, there is no strength to fight the battles that come to strengthen me to help others in my community and generation.

When I was younger, amid my first "training," I could remember a lot of spiritual things but didn't know what they meant at the time. One day, I was in the living room, and the Holy Spirit came upon me. Years before that happened, I asked my family members in church if I could receive what they had, which was the gift of tongues. At the time, when I first felt the Holy Spirit, I didn't like it. I wanted to pull away from it. I saw heavenly angels during the experience and yelled, *"Leave me alone! I don't want it!"* The feeling left me, but I still remember it to this day. It scared me then, but I came to realize it was the fear of the Lord.

The second stage of my training journey started with a big step onto the battlefield. On November 18, 2021, my father passed away suddenly. It hurt me, but I realized that it had to happen for two reasons: 1. to help my community and generation, and 2. to get my attention. I felt like dying during that battle. The enemy thought he had me—until God stepped in and delivered me.

You see, I was very depressed and suicidal. Meanwhile, my mom started following online sermons, going to church, speaking the Holy language of Jesus, and building her faith stronger. One night, she took me to a service where a prophet saw me and the demon of suicide on me. He said the following six words to me: *"I cancel the spirit of suicide."* I fell to the floor. Another prophet came and held me as she spoke tongues over me. When I finally got up, I began to see things in the spirit realm. I saw spirits leaving me and going into the ceiling. That night, I also received my gift of tongues.

The Lord delivered me from depression and suicide so that I could use my training to help others fight those same battles. At the time of this writing, it's been three years since I became strong in the Spiritual Gifts the Lord gave me to help myself and others.

For example, one time, when I came home from school, I just started screaming and crying in my room. I was so tired of everything around me. I was tired of being tired! I cried out, **_"Why, God? Why am I still here in this situation?"_** I felt the battle was so confusing and decided I wanted to give up, but I didn't realize I've got to fight for my generation.

Another time, I was riding the school bus, and my friend told me something that was going on in her life. I began to pray for her and told her it would be alright. The next day, she never complained about her situation.

Yet another time, one of my friends was getting picked on and didn't know what to do. All he knew was to fight. I told him, _"It's not them who don't like you; the demons in them_ *don't like you. Don't try to fight demons that you have the power to uproot in the name of Jesus."*

I also recall the time I was on the bus, reading about praise and turning my sadness into a glory garment of gladness (see Psalm 30:11). A younger boy caught my attention for some reason, so I shared with him what I was reading. I instructed him to read it for himself and said, *"You should praise God in any situation. Never try to fit in with the world. Instead, always fit with what is right with you and your faith."* To see that little boy reading the bible made me feel better about the battle I was facing. I was reminded of when I was his age, seeking God in the battle with no weapons, weak and curious about it all. I recalled going through things and feeling like no one could help me.

For many of us, when people make rumors about us, we get upset and want to fight or get revenge in the natural world by our own hands instead of being awakened and looking in the spiritual world where all the answers are. If we keep in mind that we have the power of the mighty Drill Sergeant—the Lord Jesus—we can uproot and destroy every demonic setup that may try to form against us and the calling the Lord has given us.

Sometimes, as a warrior, you may wonder, *"How can I fight for my generation if I'm going through some of the same things they're going through?"* I know I've felt that way before. Here's what you can do as you seek an answer to that question: Get on your knees and pray. It really is that simple! Now that I can help others, I see how all that I'd gone through— denying Christ, hurts, curiosity, etc.—as a warrior of God was used for His glory. Another thing I learned is to do what I love to do before the Lord, such as dancing, praising, singing, and drawing the things I am going through.

Doing things you love during battles can help you a lot as a warrior of Christ, as they can strengthen your faith in Him. Every time you do those things, they prepare you for the battles ahead. Keep this in mind, though: One big battle leads to the next one, but you can do **ALL** things through Christ, who will always strengthen you.

Present Yet Absent Father

BY CYNSERE WILLIAMS

Cynsere Williams

I n the United States, approximately 18.4 million children reside in a single mother household, meaning there is no father present (https://earthweb.com/fatherless-homes-statistics). As a result, many children begin acting out.

When my dad got out of the penitentiary, he already had a girlfriend, two stepchildren, and a baby on the way. I recall when a family friend visited, and my dad introduced his girlfriend's daughter as "My Lil' Princess." As for me, he simply introduced me as "his daughter."

I always wanted my dad's attention, hoping he would actually love and care about me, not just my sister. After all, he was never really there for me. We don't have the typical father-daughter relationship. I feel invisible and ignored even when I'm around my sister and him. I have since learned to advocate for myself by giving hints about what was going on, but I would always lie when asked what was wrong with me. Why did I lie? Because I felt like nobody would understand and that my feelings were "stupid." Plus, I didn't want anyone to talk bad about me like they'd done in the past.

The day came when I realized that my response to the negativity in my life was unhealthy, so I stayed quiet and spent a lot of time alone in my room. I stayed to myself and didn't want to talk to anybody. I just wanted to be alone. . . until I realized that was unhealthy, too. I decided to invest time in myself by doing a daily skin routine in the morning. Even those days when I wasn't going anywhere, I made videos to boost my self-esteem.

I also started writing in my journal to help me cope with loneliness. I also changed my diet to a healthier one because I used to always eat when I was stressed or when something went wrong. Crying also helped me at times. I figured out that it's okay to cry. Sometimes, after writing down my emotions, I would tear up the paper, burn it, or flush it down the toilet. Once that was done, I felt a little relief, but the feeling remained in my gut that something would always be wrong with me. At one point, I started going to counseling sessions but stopped shortly after that because I felt no progress was being made.

Along my self-discovery journey, I started attending an alternative school in my sixth-grade year because I was acting out. I still misbehaved at the alternative school (I stupidly made a terroristic threat that prompted a visit from the police to my home to search for weapons).

I'll start going to anger management classes soon and get a new counselor who can help me process my anger and other issues because I don't want to talk to my mom or dad about the things I'm going through. For example, I've always wanted a baby sister. My dad's girlfriend gave birth to a little girl, but I don't claim her as my sister. In fact, I don't even know her because my dad's now ex-girlfriend took her away from him. However, my mom gave me a little sister, and she is the only reason I push my way through each and every day. My little sister is the only reason I continue to write in my journal and am seeking counseling. Also, my oldest sister had a baby, which is another reason I'm taking better care of my body and mental health. I don't want my younger sister and niece to not know who I truly am. Once I realized I must do better, I cleaned up my act and started doing better!

When my dad and his girlfriend broke up, my dad came back into my life. Almost immediately, I started acting out again in school and hung out with the wrong people. I ended up getting into trouble for something I didn't have anything to do with, so they returned me to the alternative school. When I told my dad about it, he started communicating and hanging out with me more, but I still felt invisible with my sister around because they had a bond that I didn't share with him. I lashed out at my sister at one point and argued with her in front of our dad. During that argument, I had no choice but to say how I felt about everything that bothered me. Guess what? After I did that, I felt better!

Since then, I always remember that tough times don't last, but tough people do. To you, I say this: Even though things may not be the best right now, it's important to have faith that they will get better. Sometimes, things have to get worse before they can get better.

Unstoppable Radiance: Embracing Your Inner Power!

BY MCKINZIE BAKER

McKinzie Baker

When I was younger, I never saw confidence as a weakness, but I didn't see it as a strength either. In fact, I never really thought about it until I got into 4th grade. I know. . . it sounds confusing. I didn't quite understand it myself at the time. Confidence can be both good and bad. As for me, I never really cared about anyone's looks or appearance. I've never questioned myself about even having confidence because it didn't matter to me. I just thought it was a thing people called "real." Still, I had a problem with saying positive things to myself. I didn't see myself as a good or even decent-looking person; I just thought I was someone with feelings and a good heart.

Sometimes, realizing your power, strength, or worth is hard.

One thing I know is that it's hard to see yourself as an amazing person, even when others tell you all the time. It "just happens" or doesn't click, to the point you can't accept it as it is—which is something I try my hardest to look in the face and accept, but I just look and see a person who's decent like everyone else. There were times when I avoided looking in the mirror because I just knew I was decent and okay. Not good or bad, just okay. Sometimes, I'd even see other girls look in mirrors and fix their hair or faces with makeup, lip gloss, or mascara. All the time, I wish I looked like them, but I'd just leave and think, *"I shouldn't be so hard on myself because it's not good for me."*

Comparing myself to others was a part of my lack of confidence and low self-esteem.

When I entered 6th grade, my low self-esteem seemed to get even lower. I received compliments every now and then—and I was thankful—but the thoughts about myself sometimes flooded my mind.

Am I really that pretty?

Did I have a cute or cool outfit?

Is humor enough?

Does he or she think I'm nice?

Am I missing something?

It was a vicious cycle of the same thing: thoughts, feelings, and questions on repeat. I never would have thought embracing some features could be that hard in one lifetime!

Your nose. Your forehead. Your laugh. Your smile. Your confidence as it relates to those things is a reflection of what you're proud of. . . and what you're not so proud of. As for me, they were things that circled through my head, trying to help, but empowering and rebuilding your confidence can be challenging.

For starters, I tried becoming softer and kinder to myself about certain things, including my forehead, nose, hair, and any other features I could work on and improve. Even though I still receive compliments, I work to at least accept them and know someone cares about me enough to say something kind. Now, I understand that some people find it hard to accept compliments, but they say "Thank you" and go on about their day. I like to try to make daily reminders to make sure I don't feel down and low and that I can still put a smile on my face every day.

If you need a good time to start, that time is now! Don't let people walk all over you, and don't compare yourself to others who are different. Working hard to fix your broken star takes work, but you can start by pushing yourself! Try boasting about yourself more and see the beauty or handsomeness in your facial features. For example, your nose, smile, teeth, lips, eyes, skin, and other features are uniquely yours. Don't think you must have something others have because they're not you! Don't try to be someone you're not because it's unhealthy for your overall well-being and style.

I'm still trying to understand my worth. Although I'm in the 7th grade now, my self-esteem has gotten lower, but I still push through and put a smile on my face every day. I realize to show that I deserve to be a star, my outside must shine as brightly as my inside. That includes my smile, nose, lips, ears, forehead, hands, and any other thing I used to compare myself to.

It would help if you understood that people are unique. You are you, and I am me. That's just as it should be!

People like your friends may not see it, but those who feel less or not special can truly understand and know how it feels to have low self-esteem. Nonetheless, please don't compare your unique self to people who have their likings and choices of their own. You should know that people are different, and it's okay to feel like you're different because you are in a way no one could understand. Everyone is different and has their own ways of thinking and doing things, so don't be hard on yourself over a small insecurity! Do your best to feel like yourself and boost your confidence. That's the right way to begin!

You're unique. You're powerful. Your beauty or handsomeness ties it all together to make you a special person inside and out. Overall, just be yourself and love yourself, knowing that you matter to the ones around you. Don't let anything bring down your positivity. Try not to be hard on yourself. You can only do so much, which still means a lot to some people. Try being kinder to yourself, too. Sometimes, you just need to remind yourself that you are good enough and that you belong. Soon enough, doing those things will help you feel more confident and good about yourself.

How to Stand Up

BY PAIGE IVORY

Paige Ivory

How to Speak Up to a Friend

Some kids—like me—are sometimes afraid to speak up, but I'm here to tell you how it can be done.

First, you want to tell the person what they did wrong and explain why it was wrong. If they get mad at you and start to yell, try and talk to them to calm them down. If they keep yelling, then go and tell a trusted adult. They can talk to that person and work things out. After that, if they are still mad, just ignore him/her and tell your friends about the situation. Supportive friends will help you work through it.

Next, you want to figure out the best thing to say to him/her to calm them down. If they ignore you, ask one or more of your friends to try talking to that person. Make sure that your friend (or group of friends) tells you exactly what happened during the conversation. That way, you can try to understand your angry friend's point of view and figure things out. I suggest leaving them alone for at least a day or two so that they can blow off some steam and actually talk to you without getting too mad again. If you can manage to do that, you just might have a chance to save your friendship. Here's the thing, though: Be prepared to say sorry for ignoring them and for causing part of the huge fight (the other person should also apologize for the same things).

After that, if the two of you like to hug, then hug it out and continue on with your day. Tell your family and friends that you and the other person have resolved the problem. You might also want to celebrate a little bit. If so, go out for a fancy dinner or go shopping at your favorite store or the mall.

Finally, make sure that there are no more things going on between you and other friends, your parents, and siblings. If there is, work together to fix it. If there is absolutely nothing going on between you and anybody else, then enjoy life and do well in school.

Whatever life throws at you, catch it, use it, and excel at it, especially if it deals with your best friend.

How to Stand Up to Parents

Have you and your parents ever gotten into a disagreement that turned into a big argument? Well, if you have, the following steps are for you.

First, make sure all of you are on the same topic. If you're not, refocus on the original topic. Then, allow your parents to talk so that you can see their point of view. After listening to them, take your turn to speak so that your parents can see your point of view. It's likely that if they do not agree with you, they will give you their reasons and examples for their side to "win." Be prepared to share your reasons and examples so that they gain a better understanding of your position. Maybe—*just maybe*—you will win.

If, after talking, you and your parents cannot reach an agreement, try to compromise with them. That way, you will not have to argue for much longer. If you do not reach the compromising part, part ways for a little while to let each other get some fresh air and breathe for however long is necessary before trying to talk again.

At some point, you will have to decide what a compromise would look like, which might be tough for some people. Still, taking the time to think about it will often lead to the correct choice.

Finally, be the first to say sorry after the argument. Actually, you should apologize to each other because it's likely the argument wasn't even worth the time and effort, especially if you were arguing over something someone said about the other person.

If you and your parents are huggers, then hug it out. Afterward, you could ride a bike, take a nap, or play a board game together. The list goes on and on about what you could do to get your mind off the argument.

The idea here is to be creative—but be sure to include your parents!

Courageously Unbothered

BY RIGHTEOUS WILLIAMS

Righteous Williams

C hild sexual abuse is a widespread problem, as proven evident by the following statistic: *"One in 9 girls and 1 in 20 boys under the age of 18 experience sexual abuse or assault. 82% of all victims under 18 are female"* (rainn.org/statistics/children-and-teens).

I was six the first time I was sexually assaulted. Of course, I didn't understand what was happening to me at that age. In fact, I was still confused about my dad being arrested and locked away. For years on end, I was taught that "it" was a game and something that families did to show love for one another. Over eight years later, I officially decided to come out about the experience.

Years of self-hate, anger, depression, self-harming, eating disorders, Post-Traumatic Stress Disorder (PTSD), anxiety, body dysmorphia, and fake smiles were finally overcome by the telling of my truth. For many years, I was stuck in a mental lock because I was confused, scared, and just numb. All the while, my family thought I was miserable for no good reason. Most people around me assumed I was okay because I always had a smile plastered on my face. For a while, it felt like I had kept myself muted.

Much like all children, I learned certain things that led to me living my life based on the rules I was taught to follow. A few of those rules included:

- Not telling anyone what was happening to me;
- Always obey; and
- Change my appearance to how "they" wanted me to be seen, only around "them."

Initially, I was treated kindly and given many compliments, but after "they" got comfortable abusing me, I would be insulted about my weight and appearance. I was always either too nice or too mean. I had to change my personality so often as a child that even to this day—as a teen—I get confused trying to figure out who I am. Even in school, I felt compelled to please everyone because it was what I was used to doing. Although I knew the things being done to me were wrong, I was okay with it. . . as long as "they" left my sister alone. I could only stop so much, though. I was too young and defenseless as it was.

The time finally came when I broke mentally. I was always angry, always had an attitude, and never wanted to eat. I had completely lost control of my personality and started smoking and drinking. I felt compelled to "grow up fast" because I wanted to be an adult since I never had the chance just to be a kid.

The day I came out about everything, I was sitting in a therapist's office (the 5th one I'd had so far). As I was being evaluated, I noted that it was the first time someone asked me **directly**, "Have you ever been sexually assaulted or abused?" I was taken aback at that moment because I didn't know what to say or do. Noticing how uncomfortable I was, the therapist asked my mother to leave the room. Once again, the therapist asked the same question: "Have you ever been sexually assaulted or abused?" I replied that I had and was then asked to describe in detail what had occurred, which proved difficult because I had the image of my mother's angry face as she left the room, taking up space in my head. Knowing that she was so upset only served to make me angrier.

Up until that moment in the therapist's office, I sometimes spoke about the experience I endured to others, which was followed by me trying to push the memories out of my head. Sadly, I'll never forget the first time I was touched inappropriately, especially since it was not consensual.

When you've grown accustomed to doing a specific thing constantly, it becomes second nature—like eating and sleeping—and begins to feel like something you need. As for me, I felt like I needed to please everyone and make them happy. So, whenever I disappointed someone or made them mad, I became more frustrated and angrier.

Seeing my mother so distraught made me close off more. I could say what happened to me in great detail, but I could never actually speak about how it affected me or how I felt. I swore to myself to keep silent, but things around me began to change: people were more patient with me, less angry at me, didn't yell at me as much, and were calmer with me. It didn't change my mentality concerning the situation, but it did make me feel more at ease. Sometimes, I still feel like something is mentally wrong with me, but I'm still working on myself.

Before I came out about the situation, volunteering and giving made me feel at ease. Although I couldn't please everyone, I made sure to please the ones I could. After finally speaking about what happened to me, my mind doesn't always feel as foggy. I still feel the need to grow up faster, but I've learned to put a pause on that desire and allow myself to be a teen while I can. I'm still not very good at eating, but I eat more than before. There are times when I starve myself, but I quickly get myself back on track. I still have pretty bad insomnia, but I'm also working on getting better sleep, which is challenging at times because those bad things happened to me during that night (perhaps that's why I'm now such a "night owl").

Mentally, my mind is still on lockdown. In person, I'm a loud and bubbly character who has somehow learned to be more vocal and expressive about my feelings. I'm not very good at it yet, but I'm getting there! My prior anger issues have simmered to a slight irritation. I used to try and have as many friends as possible, but I'm practically a popular loner now. Being alone hurts sometimes, but I try to constantly remind myself that I'm a human who needs a break, needs to learn to love herself, and needs to learn how to be at peace within her own body.

If there was one piece of advice I would give to young ladies, in particular, who have been sexually assaulted or abused, it would be this: Do not blame yourself. I know people say that a lot, but it is meant to help you.

I blamed myself for not saying anything for so long. I always felt like if I had, my sister would not have been affected, but I was still a child. . . I was still lost.

Don't blame yourself because, no matter what anyone says, you didn't ask for those things to happen to you. Allow yourself to grow. You may not forget, but you must forgive—not for them, but for yourself. Forgiveness is the first step to self-love and inner peace. Don't drown in self-pity or doubt. We are all humans. We all go through pain. We all suffer at times, but we decide for ourselves whether or not we grow as people. We determine our happiness. Never allow yourself to forget that.

In closing, I leave you with these words:

"Bearing with one another and, if one has a complaint against another, forgiving each other; as the Lord has forgiven you, so you also must forgive" (Colossians 3:13).

AFTERWORD

Congratulations on finishing this incredible book written by eight extraordinary young individuals! Their stories are not only a testament to their resilience and strength but also a source of inspiration for countless others who may be going through similar challenges in their lives. As we come to the end of this book, it's important to reflect on the significant impact these youths have made on the lives of their peers.

Impact of the Youths' Stories

The stories shared in this book are a powerful reminder that everyone faces their own battles and that no one is alone in their struggles. These eight youths have shown incredible courage in opening up about their experiences, and in doing so, they have created a supportive community where others can find solace and understanding. Their words have the potential to bring comfort, hope, and strength to those who may be feeling lost or isolated.

Each story is a beacon of light, guiding others through the darkness, and reminding them that there is always a way forward. Through their honesty and vulnerability, these young authors have become beacons of hope for their peers, showing that it's okay to speak up, seek help, and never lose faith in a brighter tomorrow.

A Message to Parents and Guardians

To the parents and guardians of these incredible youths, we extend our deepest gratitude for nurturing and supporting them on their journey to sharing their stories. Your role in shaping their confidence, resilience, and empathy cannot be overstated. As these young individuals continue to grow and evolve, it's important to provide them with the guidance and support they need to keep sharing their stories and extending help to others during their formative years.

Here are a few tips to effectively nurture and support your youth in continuing to share their stories and extend help to others:

- **Encourage Open Communication:** Do so by creating an environment where open and honest conversations are welcomed. Let your youth know that they can always talk to you about anything without fear of judgment.

- **Provide Emotional Support:** Validate their feelings and experiences and offer emotional support when they need it. Your understanding and empathy can make a world of difference in their willingness to share and help others.

- **Empower Them:** Encourage their passions and interests and empower them to use their experiences to create positive change. Help them find platforms to share their stories and connect with others who may benefit from their wisdom.

- **Seek Professional Help if Needed:** If you notice signs of distress or struggle in your youth, don't hesitate to seek professional help. Mental health professionals can provide the support and guidance needed to navigate through difficult times.

In Conclusion. . .

The impact of these young authors goes beyond the pages of this book. They have ignited a spark of hope and resilience in the hearts of their peers and have shown that through unity and understanding, we can overcome even the toughest of challenges.

As we bring *Impact Generation: Youth Activism for a Better Tomorrow to a close*, let's remember to continue supporting and uplifting the voices of our youth, for they are the storytellers and advocates of tomorrow.

With warmest regards,

Angela R. Edwards, Compiler

SCRIPTURES AND ACTIVITIES FOR TODAY'S YOUTH

You are encouraged to use the following scriptures and activities to help you get through each day—especially the challenging ones—while learning something new.

There are 20 passages of scripture included, followed by fun and engaging activities to spur your imagination and motivate you to use your intellect!

Be sure to include your family and friends, no matter their age!

Enjoy!

Scriptures - Navigating Challenging Days

1. **Psalm 46:1**
   - "God is our refuge and strength, an ever-present help in trouble."
   - Implement: Start your day by reflecting on this verse. Remind yourself that you can find strength and refuge in your faith, especially during challenging times.

2. **Isaiah 41:10**
   - "So do not fear, for I am with you; do not be dismayed, for I am your God. I will strengthen you and help you; I will uphold you with my righteous right hand."
   - Implement: Whenever you feel anxious or discouraged, recite this verse as a source of comfort and assurance.

3. **Philippians 4:13**
   - "I can do all this through him who gives me strength."
   - Implement: Use this verse as a daily affirmation, reminding yourself that you have the strength to overcome any challenges with faith.

4. Psalm 34:17-18

- "The righteous cry out, and the Lord hears them; he delivers them from all their troubles. The Lord is close to the brokenhearted and saves those who are crushed in spirit."

- Implement: Meditate on these verses during moments of distress, finding solace in the belief that God is attentive to your pain and offers deliverance.

5. Romans 8:28

- "And we know that in all things God works for the good of those who love him, who have been called according to his purpose."

- Implement: Reflect on this verse as a reminder that even in difficult circumstances, there is a purpose and potential for good to emerge.

6. Joshua 1:9

- "Have I not commanded you? Be strong and courageous. Do not be afraid; do not be discouraged, for the Lord your God will be with you wherever you go."

- Implement: Carry this verse with you as a source of courage and encouragement, especially when facing uncertainties or challenges.

7. **Psalm 23:4**
   - "Even though I walk through the darkest valley, I will fear no evil, for you are with me; your rod and your staff, they comfort me."
   - Implement: Recite this verse as a reminder that God's presence brings comfort and reassurance, even in the midst of difficult times.

8. **Proverbs 3:5-6**
   - "Trust in the Lord with all your heart and lean not on your own understanding; in all your ways submit to him, and he will make your paths straight."
   - Implement: Use this verse as a guide for decision-making and surrendering worries, trusting that God will direct your path.

9. **Matthew 11:28**
   - "Come to me, all you who are weary and burdened, and I will give you rest."

- Implement: When feeling overwhelmed, turn to this verse for the promise of finding rest and relief in God's presence.

10. Lamentations 3:22-23

- "Because of the Lord's great love we are not consumed, for his compassions never fail. They are new every morning; great is your faithfulness."
- Implement: Start each day with gratitude, reflecting on God's faithfulness and love, which offer renewal and hope.

11. Psalm 55:22

- "Cast your cares on the Lord and he will sustain you; he will never let the righteous be shaken."
- Implement: Make a habit of surrendering your worries and burdens to God, trusting in His promise to sustain and uphold you.

12. 2 Corinthians 4:16-18

- "Therefore we do not lose heart. Though outwardly we are wasting away, yet inwardly we are being renewed day by day. For our light and momentary troubles are achieving for us an eternal glory that far outweighs them all. So we fix our eyes not on what is seen, but on what is unseen, since what is seen is temporary, but what is unseen is eternal."

- Implement: Reflect on this verse to gain a perspective that transcends temporary challenges, focusing on the eternal hope and renewal found in faith.

13. **1 Peter 5:7**
    - "Cast all your anxiety on him because he cares for you."
    - Implement: Practice letting go of anxiety by entrusting your concerns to God, knowing that He cares for you deeply.

14. **Psalm 30:5**
    - "Weeping may stay for the night, but rejoicing comes in the morning."
    - Implement: Embrace the hope offered in this verse, recognizing that difficult times are temporary, and joy will ultimately prevail.

15. Hebrews 13:5

- "Keep your lives free from the love of money and be content with what you have, because God has said, 'Never will I leave you; never will I forsake you.'"
- Implement: Use this verse as a reminder of God's unchanging presence and find contentment in His faithfulness.

16. James 1:2-4

- "Consider it pure joy, my brothers and sisters, whenever you face trials of many kinds, because you know that the testing of your faith produces perseverance. Let perseverance finish its work so that you may be mature and complete, not lacking anything."
- Implement: View challenges as opportunities for growth and maturity, drawing strength from the potential for perseverance and spiritual development.

17. Psalm 121:1-2

- "I lift up my eyes to the mountains— where does my help come from? My help comes from the Lord, the Maker of heaven and earth."

- Implement: Turn to this verse during moments of uncertainty, finding reassurance in the unwavering support and guidance of God.

18. Romans 15:13

- "May the God of hope fill you with all joy and peace as you trust in him, so that you may overflow with hope by the power of the Holy Spirit."
- Implement: Seek hope and peace by meditating on this verse, inviting the presence of God to fill you with joy and assurance.

19. Psalm 62:5-8

- "Yes, my soul, find rest in God; my hope comes from him. Truly he is my rock and my salvation; he is my fortress, I will not be shaken. My salvation and my honor depend on God; he is my mighty rock, my refuge. Trust in him at all times, you people; pour out your hearts to him, for God is our refuge."
- Implement: Embrace this verse as a source of rest and stability, anchoring your trust and hope in God's unwavering strength.

20. John 14:27

- "Peace I leave with you; my peace I give you. I do not give to you as the world gives. Do not let your hearts be troubled and do not be afraid."
- Implement: Carry this verse with you as a reminder of the peace that surpasses worldly understanding, finding solace in the gift of peace offered through faith.

You are encouraged to reflect on those scriptures regularly, integrating them into your daily routine by reading, reciting, or meditating on them during challenging moments. Each verse offers comfort, strength, and guidance, serving as a source of hope and assurance in difficult times.

ALIAS ADVENTURE

Instructions: Spelling out your first name, assign the following corresponding word to those letters.

For example, JAY would be: J-Joyful, A-Amazing, Y-Youthful

Amazing, Bold, Creative, Daring, Energetic, Fun-loving, Genuine, Hopeful, Imaginative, Joyful, Kind-hearted, Lively, Motivated, Nurturing, Outgoing, Passionate, Quirky, Resilient, Spirited, Tenacious, Unique, Vibrant, Witty, Xenial, Youthful, Zealous

_____

_____

_____

_____

_____

_____

CROSSWORD PUZZLE

Impact Generation Expressions

Across

[1] To do something exceptionally well or to look amazing.
[6] Used to describe something exciting, amazing, or very cool.
[7] Something that spreads rapidly on the internet, like a popular video or meme.
[9] Someone who has a large following on social media and can impact trends and opinions.
[11] A word used to describe someone who is attractive or appealing.
[12] Someone who is overly attentive, submissive, or accommodating to someone they like.
[14] A term of endearment for your significant other or crush.
[15] To show off or boast about something, often related to achievements or possessions.
[16] To be aware of social issues and injustices.

Down

[1] Your close group of friends who always have your back.
[2] An exclamation used to express excitement or triumph.
[3] Used to describe something cool or fierce.
[4] A significant improvement in someone's appearance or style.
[5] A photo you take of yourself, often to share on social media.
[8] A popular app for creating and sharing short videos.
[10] Used to describe something or someone you aspire to be like.
[11] Your close group of friends who always have your back.
[13] A funny image, video, or piece of text that is shared widely online.
[15] Fear Of Missing Out, the anxiety that something exciting is happening elsewhere.

CROSSWORD PUZZLE SOLUTION

WHAT KIND OF CREATIVE ARE YOU?

Question 1:

When are you most inspired to create something new?

- a) Late at night, when everything is quiet, and I can focus.
- b) When I'm surrounded by nature and fresh air.
- c) In the middle of a bustling city, where there's so much to see and experience.
- d) When I'm with my friends or family, bouncing ideas off each other.

Question 2:

Which of these activities sounds most appealing to you?

- a) Painting or drawing something from my imagination.
- b) Writing a story or poem that evokes strong emotions.
- c) Composing music or experimenting with different sounds.

- d) Planning and hosting an event or gathering for a cause I believe in.

Question 3:

What's your favorite way to express yourself?
- a) Through visual art - colors, shapes, and textures speak to me.
- b) Through words - I love crafting stories, lyrics, or powerful messages.
- c) Through music - creating melodies and rhythms is my thing.
- d) Through organizing and bringing people together for a common purpose.

Question 4:

Which of these creative environments would you thrive in?
- a) A cozy art studio with natural light and lots of space to work.
- b) A quiet nook with a desk and a view, perfect for writing and reflecting.
- c) A music studio filled with various instruments and recording equipment.

- d) A collaborative space where I can brainstorm and work with others.

Question 5:

What inspires you the most?
- a) The beauty of the world around me and the emotions it evokes.
- b) Stories of people's experiences, struggles, and triumphs.
- c) Different genres of music and the way they make me feel.
- d) Making a positive impact and creating change in my community.

Question 6:

Which of these activities do you find most enjoyable?
- a) Experimenting with different art mediums and techniques.
- b) Getting lost in a captivating book or writing my thoughts.
- c) Playing an instrument or composing melodies.
- d) Organizing events, volunteering, or leading a group project.

Question 7:

What do you value most in your creative pursuits?
- a) The ability to convey emotions and ideas visually.
- b) The power of storytelling and connecting with others through words.
- c) The freedom and expression found in creating music and sound.
- d) The opportunity to inspire and unite people through collaborative projects.

Question 8:

What role do you usually take in group projects or activities?
- a) The visionary - I come up with the overall concept or design.
- b) The storyteller - I craft the narrative or message.
- c) The musician - I create the soundtrack or set the mood.
- d) The organizer - I bring people together and make things happen.

Results:

Count how many times you chose each letter:

- Mostly a's: You're a Visual Artist! Your creativity shines through colors, shapes, and visual expressions.
- Mostly b's: You're a Wordsmith! Your strength lies in storytelling, writing, and conveying emotions through words.
- Mostly c's: You're a Sound Maestro! Your creativity thrives through music, sound, and rhythm.
- Mostly d's: You're a Community Creator! Your passion lies in bringing people together and organizing collaborative projects to make a positive impact.

Each type of creativity is essential and brings something unique to the table. Embrace your creative strengths and keep exploring the world of possibilities!

MINDFULNESS EXERCISES, MEDITATION TECHNIQUES, AND RELAXATION ACTIVITIES FOR TEENS

Mindfulness Exercises

1. **Deep Breathing**
   - Find a comfortable spot and take slow, deep breaths for several minutes. Inhale deeply through your nose, hold for a few seconds, and exhale slowly through your mouth. Focus on the sensation of your breath entering and leaving your body.

2. **Body Scan**
   - Lie down or sit comfortably. Close your eyes and mentally scan your body from head to toe, focusing on each part and noticing any tension or sensations. Release any tension you find as you breathe.

3. Mindful Walking
   - Take a leisurely walk and pay attention to each step. Notice the sensations in your feet as they touch the ground, the movement of your legs, and the environment around you. Stay present and observe without judgment.

Meditation Techniques

1. Guided Meditation Apps
   - Use meditation apps designed for teens, which offer guided sessions focused on stress relief, self-compassion, and relaxation. Set aside a few minutes daily for guided meditation.

2. Visualization Meditation
   - Close your eyes and imagine a peaceful place, such as a beach or a forest. Visualize the sights, sounds, and feelings of being there, allowing yourself to relax and let go of stress.

3. Breath Counting
   - Sit quietly and focus on your breath. Count each inhalation and exhalation, aiming to reach a count of 10. If your mind wanders, gently bring

your focus back to your breath and start counting again.

Relaxation Activities

1. **Yoga**
   - Follow beginner-friendly yoga videos or join a local class. Yoga helps improve flexibility, reduce stress, and promote relaxation through gentle movement and focused breathing.

2. **Nature Walks**
   - Spend time in nature by going for a hike, visiting a park, or simply taking a walk in a natural setting. Notice the sounds, smells, and sights around you, allowing nature to soothe your mind.

3. **Art Therapy**
   - Engage in art activities like coloring, painting, or sketching. Use this time to express yourself creatively and let go of stress through artistic expression.

4. Journaling

- Write about your thoughts, feelings, and experiences in a journal. Reflect on positive moments, express gratitude, and release any worries onto the pages.

5. Digital Detox

- Take a break from screens and digital devices for a set period each day. Use this time to engage in offline activities, connect with loved ones, or simply be present in the moment.

Encourage yourself to explore these activities and find what works best for you. Remember: Taking care of your mental well-being is important. Implementing at least one of those exercises can help you manage stress and promote a healthy, balanced life.

MINDFULNESS EXERCISES – INTEGRATION TIPS

1. **Set Reminders**
   - Use your phone or a planner to schedule specific times for mindfulness exercises, meditation, or relaxation activities. Setting reminders can help you prioritize self-care amidst your daily routine.

2. **Start Small**
   - Begin with just a few minutes each day for these activities. Gradually increase the duration as you become more comfortable. Consistency is key, so aim for regular practice rather than lengthy sessions.

3. **Create a Relaxation Space**
   - Designate a quiet, comfortable space in your room or home where you can practice mindfulness and relaxation. Personalize it with calming decor, cushions, or soothing lighting to make it an inviting atmosphere.

4. Incorporate Mindfulness into Daily Tasks

- Practice mindfulness while doing everyday tasks like eating, showering, or walking to school. Focus on the sensations and experiences of these activities, using them as opportunities for mindfulness.

5. Join a Group

- Consider joining a yoga class, meditation group, or nature walking club with friends or classmates. Having a supportive community can make these activities more enjoyable and encourage consistency.

6. Morning or Evening Ritual

- Integrate mindfulness or meditation into your morning or evening routine. Starting or ending the day with these practices can set a positive tone and help you manage stress throughout the day.

7. Experiment and Adapt

- Explore different activities and techniques to find what resonates most with you. Adapt these practices to suit your preferences and lifestyle, making them a natural part of your daily routine.

Finding time for self-care and well-being is essential for managing stress and nurturing your mental health. By integrating these activities into your daily routine, you can cultivate a wholesome, well-adjusted lifestyle.

SCRIPT SCRAMBLE

Correctly unscramble the following words. Don't cheat!

UAISMTBOI _____

REACRE _____

EHCRE _____

IETVAERC _____

CADNE _____

TNOOEIMS _____

FASHOIN _____

IRIPSFHNED _____

CUSMI _____

ILONNE _____

POTAISSEAN _____

NRPISOLAIHETS _____

OATXEALNIR _____

EOASBDKGTRNIA _____

STRAM _____

SRESSDET _____

HUESNNIS _____

ELDATENT _____

Script Scramble Solution

UAISMTBOI	AMBITIOUS
REACRE	CAREER
EHCRE	CHEER
IETVAERC	CREATIVE
CADNE	DANCE
TNOOEIMS	EMOTIONS
FASHOIN	FASHION
IRIPSFHNED	FRIENDSHIP
CUSMI	MUSIC
ILONNE	ONLINE
POTAISSEAN	PASSIONATE
NRPISOLAIHETS	RELATIONSHIPS
OATXEALNIR	RELAXATION
EOASBDKGTRNIA	SKATEBOARDING
STRAM	SMART
SRESSDET	STRESSED
HUESNNIS	SUNSHINE
ELDATENT	TALENTED

Made in the USA
Columbia, SC
17 May 2024

35827906R00050